AUSTRALIA

This book is an introduction to the land "down under" which has winter when we have summer, night when we have day; a land with snowy mountain peaks where a vast hydroelectric scheme is being developed; a land of fierce and hostile desert, of diamonds and pearls, of sheep and cattle ranches, of kangaroos and laughing birds called kookaburras.

It is also a land of exciting people. We meet early pioneers who blazed their way over mountains to discover gold and fought for their rights to it. We learn how a tough, independent democracy was born in the goldfields and how the pioneer spirit persists today. We visit remote homesteads where runways are as commonplace as our driveways, and meet the flying doctors and mailmen who land there. We watch a *corroboree,* a campfire dance of Australia's Aborigines, a people whom the government is trying to help keep their ancient arts, yet learn to live in the modern world.

When it comes time to fly home, we leave with the feeling that the future of this only country that takes up an entire continent will be "dinky dye," the Australian way of saying "A-okay."

About the Author

MARGARET PARKE, Professor of Education at Brooklyn College, traveled 8,000 miles in Australia during the nine months she spent there as a Fulbright lecturer attached to the University of Sydney. Now a teacher of teachers, she has herself taught at all levels: elementary, secondary and college, in city and country schools. She is the author of several other books for children in early grades, as well as articles in magazines for teachers.

She was born in Mauch Chunk, Pennsylvania, which changed its name to Jim Thorpe. She lives with her husband in New York City where she is a member of the Women's Press Club and the Women's National Book Association.

About the Illustrator

CLAUDINE NANKIVEL grew up in an artists' colony in Englewood, New Jersey; then studied at the Art Students' League in New York, as well as in Paris and Fontainebleau. She has also illustrated *Getting to Know Hong Kong* and *Getting to Know the Two Chinas*.

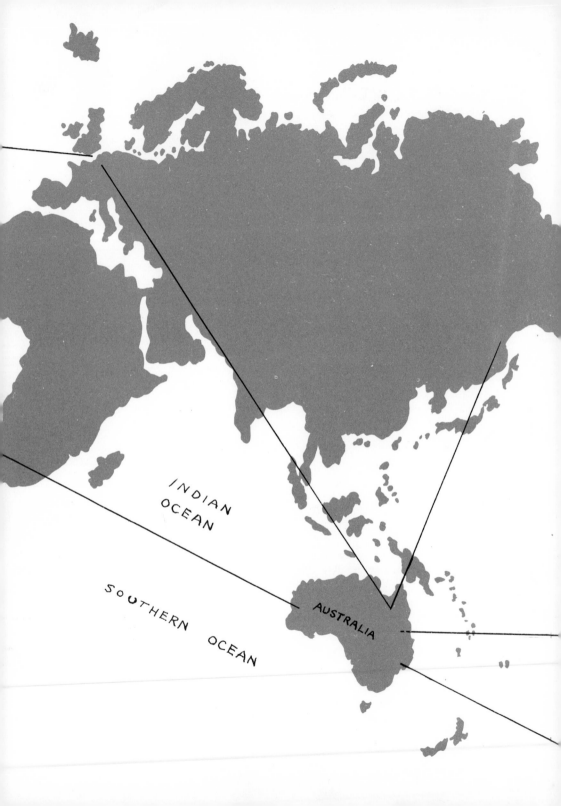

INDIAN
OCEAN

SOUTHERN OCEAN

AUSTRALIA

Getting to Know
AUSTRALIA

by MARGARET B. PARKE

Illustrated by CLAUDINE NANKIVEL

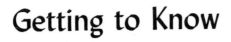

PACIFIC
OCEAN

ATLANTIC
OCEAN

COWARD-McCANN, Inc.   NEW YORK

Acknowledgments

The author wishes to express special gratitude to the United States Government for a Fulbright Grant, and to Geoffrey Rossiter, the administrator of the Fulbright Program in Australia; colleagues on the staff of the University of Sydney, especially Professor William Connell and Dr. Joyce Wylie, for their help in planning and their continued guidance; students in the graduate class in Curriculum Construction and Theory who took responsibility for introducing her to the activities in which they were engaged; the Asian students on the Colombo Plan and seminar groups; leaders in the public school system, inspectors, headmasters, and teachers; the many Australians who so graciously took her into their homes; Qantas Airlines, and the Government Travel Bureau of New South Wales for their efficiency in arranging travel details; the Australian Information and News Bureau in New York for assistance with the details needed in the preparation of this book and for their review of it; Harry Kellerman, headmaster of the Blackfriars Correspondence School, for permission to use the poem "Rain" from the *Outpost,* December 1958, p. 49.

© 1962 by Coward-McCann, Inc.

Library of Congress Catalog Card Number: 62-14907

MANUFACTURED IN THE UNITED STATES OF AMERICA

Editor of this series: Sabra Holbrook

To the many children whom I met in Australian homes and schools who helped me look at life through their eyes, this book is affectionately dedicated.

NEW GUINEA

INDIAN OCEAN

PACIFIC OCEAN

GREAT BARRIER REEF

GREAT DIVIDING RANGE

DARWIN

MT. ISA
MARY KATHLEEN

QUEENSLAND

GREAT
AUSTRALIAN
BASIN

BRISBANE

NORTHERN
TERRITORY

ALICE
SPRINGS

NEW SOUTH WALES

SYDNEY

CO
CA

BROOME

AUSTRALIA

DARLING RIVER

MURRUMBIDGEE
RIVER

M K
CA

DESERT

SOUTH

MURRAY RIVER

SNOWY RIVER

VICTORIA

MELBOURNE

YARR
RIVE

WESTERN
AUSTRALIA

ADELAIDE

HOBA

TASMANIA

PERTH

SOUTHERN OCEAN

AN ASTRONAUT, circling the earth at terrific speed, can't be sure of the boundaries of any one country until he sights the largest of all islands in the world. Then, without hesitation, he can exclaim, "Australia! The continent with only one country on it!"

That huge mass of land, south of the equator between the Indian and Pacific Oceans, is almost as large as the mainland of the United States. To the north is the island of New Guinea on which Australia governs a territory for the United Nations. To the south is the small, heart-shaped island of Tasmania. It is part of Australia. Farther to the south, Australian explorers and scientists are at work in a section of cold, frozen Antarctica.

Australia means "southland," but many call it the land *down under*. That's another way of saying it's almost halfway around the world from you and on the other side of the equator. It's winter there when you have summer, and night when you have day.

Australia is the only continent not covered by ice that is entirely in the Southern Hemisphere, the southern half of the earth. Australians' closest neighbors are the people of New Zealand and southeast Asia.

The continent was shaped by mighty forces. It broke off from the Asian mainland hundreds of millions of years ago. Then the earth heaved, and ridges of mountains rose in the center, in the south, and along the eastern coast. Volcanoes burst forth in the southeast. A tableland pushed up in the west. The sea rushed from the north into a great central basin formed by the surrounding mountains.

When the level of the water sank during the ice ages, primitive men and marsupial animals, like kangaroos which carry their young in pouches, may have walked into Australia. They could have come over bridges of land from the north and northwest. Then the roaring sea rose again, and the land bridges disappeared.

There were the animals and men, left in a secret spot by the all-encircling waters, shut away from all other life on the face of the earth. There they were to develop separately and more slowly than in any other place on earth. That's why today you find in Australia animals found nowhere else in the world, and plant life which has survived from prehistoric times.

The once-great mountains have been worn down by winds and rain, until now they are only a little higher than the Appalachian Mountains in eastern United States. Besides scattered, central ranges, the Great Dividing Range runs down the east coast, then turns parallel to the southeast coast, where it becomes the Australian Alps. In these mountains rises Australia's biggest river, the 1,500-mile-long Murray. The Darling and Murrumbidgee join it before it empties into the Southern Ocean.

The sea that once covered the great central basin has evaporated, leaving only beds of salt. In time of rain, raging torrents suddenly appear in the basin. Afterward they disappear into the earth just as quickly as they came. However, when drills are sunk, the water gushes up again like water in an artesian well. The basin is called the Great Artesian Basin.

To the west of it, covering more than a third of the continent, a sun-scorched desert rises to a height of 1,000 feet and extends all the way to the west coast. Neither man nor animal can live there long. Another third is semidesert.

In the northern lowlands and jungles there is also intense heat, but not the dry kind. The land is swept by monsoons — high winds that bring heavy rain. In the snow-covered southern mountains, there is extreme cold. Along the balmy eastern and southern coasts the climate is the best. In all, Australia has 12,000 miles of coastline.

Early map makers called Australia *Terra Incognita,* or Land Unknown. Sailors passed it by. The shores they sighted were unattractive and forbidding. Nobody wanted this continent! It was the last one to be discovered by civilized man, except for those covered by ice.

In April, 1770, Captain Cook, a British explorer, sighted the east coast of Australia and told of a delightful climate, strange plants and animals, and beautiful forests. The British Government then laid claim to the land.

After the American Revolution, the British decided to start a colony in Australia. They needed a place to send the overflow of prisoners they had been shipping to America. On January 26, 1778, more than a thousand settlers arrived in eleven ships after a long and weary trip of eight months. A small band of slim, dark-skinned men, with mops of dusky hair and smoky eyes, stood on the cliffs as the settlers approached Sydney Cove. They waved their spears and shouted, "Warra, warra!" Their cries meant, "Go away," but the settlers had come to stay.

It wasn't easy for them. All Australian nature seemed upside down to the British settlers. A wind from the south was cold, not warm as in England. Animals carried their young in pouches. Cheeky birds imitated and even laughed at the struggling colonists. Trees lost their bark instead of their leaves. The sun was in the north in the middle of the day, and at night the sky was far more brilliant than they had ever seen. Even formations of stars in the sky were different, for the five stars of the Southern Cross can be seen only south of the equator. The silence of the night was often interrupted by the cries of the Aborigines, the people whom the settlers found there — the original Australians.

Ships had to bring supplies from faraway England. Each time they came, they brought more convicts and free men as well. Six colonies were founded. In the next twenty-five years the settlers blazed their way over the mountains. They were searching for plains for the cattle and sheep they had bred from a few they brought with them. Through trackless bush, over rivers and creeks, the pioneers moved on with their animals. When they found places they liked, they cut down trees and put up bark huts. This was called *squatting,* because they just stayed or squatted there.

Until 1840, however, no one tried to find out what lay in the center of the land. Then daring men began to pack their bags for adventure into the unmapped areas of central Australia. As the adventurers shaded their eyes to look into the great wilderness beyond, the wise old Aborigines shook their heads and said in pidgin English, "Never, never." The wilderness came to be known as "Never-Never Land."

It was a land of salty swamps, intense heat, hot sand, bare bones and spinifex grass that looks and feels like porcupine needles. Two explorers, Robert Burke and William Wills, finally won the title of the first to cross it — but "never-never" did they return. They perished of hunger and thirst.

However, in the north, some adventurers also found land that was rich and fertile. When settlers heard about it, some of them began to move there with their animals. They learned to trade with the Aborigines just as the early settlers in America traded with the Indians. In exchange for land, they gave the natives knives, scissors, hatchets, blankets, mirrors, shirts, jackets and flour.

Very early, these settlers discovered that they could produce a high quality of wool. Their sheep grew finer and longer fleeces than sheep in most other countries. England needed their wool for new machines that had just been invented, which could make cloth faster than handweavers. Sheep raising grew to a profitable business.

Then came an even more profitable discovery: gold!

A great rush for gold began. Sometimes a digger would be lucky enough to scoop up 10,000 dollars' worth of the precious metal in a day. All told, the first gold strikes were worth about a billion dollars. When deposits gave out in the east, there was another great find in the west. There, the desert turned out two billion dollars' worth of gold and is still producing.

Men fought for their rights in the goldfields. When the British tried to tax gold hunters for use of the land, the diggers fought and won a bloody battle at a place called Eureka Stockade. To be known as a Eureka digger became an honor. "Digger" is still a complimentary Australian name today.

After Eureka, the British took it easier with their faraway Australian colonists. A tough, independent democracy was being born. To it, the gold brought more people — the workers to help build a nation. From 300,000, the population grew to a million in a couple of decades.

By this time the six colonies were well established. They were in New South Wales, Victoria, Tasmania, South Australia, Western Australia and Queensland. These are the names of the Australian states today. After many meetings and much talking, the six agreed to have a federal government. A government belonging to several states, which is what federal government means, attends to affairs that one big government can do better than several small ones. For example, it defends the country, and settles disputes that go beyond state boundaries. It takes care of relations with other countries.

Australians modeled their constitution on that of the United States, but kept a strong tie with the British form of government. Instead of an elected President, they accepted the British Queen as their official head. That's why a Governor General, the Queen's representative, signs the laws proposed by Parliament. The real power lies with the Parliament, the lawmaking body.

From its members, the Prime Minister chooses his ministers or cabinet. The leader of the political party that elects the most members becomes prime minister. If the doings of the ministers don't suit the majority of Parliament, the ministers must resign. Otherwise, they serve for three years.

Australia's first Federal Parliament was held in Melbourne in 1901. It represented less than 4 million people. Today the government of Australia represents more than 10 million. Yet, this still isn't very many to live in a land almost as big as our own, is it? There are over 18 times as many of us. A main reason for the big difference in population is Australia's great desert. Not yet can people live there, though someday perhaps they will. Plans are under way to beat the desert and make it habitable.

The rest of the continent is a lively, modern country. Factories stand where the first settlers hacked through scrub and bush. Farmers move their tractors and harvesters across the land once worked with wooden plow and reaping hook. Great roads stretch over the tracks made by squatters and their animals. Buses and lorries — that is, trucks — replace teams of horses and stagecoaches of days gone by. Trains carry passengers north and south, east and west, and planes crisscross the skies where early settlers saw only stars.

This land which lay unknown for such a long time has come to be among leaders in the world's struggle for peace and mutual protection. Australia helped draft the charter for the United Nations and has continued to support it strongly. Australia also played a leading role in organizing and carrying out the Colombo Plan. Named for the capital of Ceylon, where the idea for the plan was born, it tries to help people in southern Asia build roads, schools, hospitals and factories.

Australia is also a partner in SEATO, the South East Asia Treaty Organization, in which the United States and several Asian, Pacific and European countries have agreed to help each other in case of enemy attack.

In contact with many of the world's peoples, Australians have borrowed some foreign ways and inherited some others from their British ancestors. But they have developed many special ways of their own. Certain expressions of speech brand an Australian in any part of the world. A hundred per cent Australian is a *dinkum Aussie*. When everything is going well, it's *dinky dye*. A *buster* is a sudden strong wind, and a *billabong* is the water left in a stream bed when most of the stream has dried up.

You must be careful in asking for what you want. If you want a melonlike fruit called papaya, ask for *pawpaws*. If you want to go to the second floor of a building, request that the *lift* — elevator — take you to the first floor. Your first floor is ground floor to them. With a little patience, you'll soon be on speaking terms.

To get to know these people you will want to travel into all parts of their country. From California, you reach it by jet in less than a day.

As your plane descends toward the Sydney airport, you look down on a harbor crowded with boats. There are all kinds, from great liners to tiny rowboats. Many are yachts. Red-roofed bungalows, apartment houses, beautiful parks and beaches border the blue waters of the spacious harbor. A multitude of homes covers the surrounding hills at all levels.

Your plane touches ground, skims to a stop, and there are Kathy and Peter to greet you. They have come to take you to one of the harbor homes you saw on the cliff as your plane was landing.

Traffic jams, the rush of people to and from buses and trains, ferry traffic on the bay, attractive stores and shopping centers make it hard to believe that you are out of the United States and down under. You recognize so much that seems familiar. An occasional sign in a store window which reads WELCOME, AMERICAN GOODS! assures you that you really are away from home.

Today is Easter Sunday, and many people are coming home from church. Free to worship God as they please, Australians go to churches of different denominations — for instance, the Church of England, the Roman Catholic, Methodist, Presbyterian, Baptist, Congregational churches. The Jewish people attended their synagogues yesterday.

The children are on Easter vacation now, and you are surprised to learn that Easter Monday is a holiday as well as Sunday. So is the day after Christmas, which they call Boxing Day. Long ago, in England, Christmas boxes were given on this day, but now around Sydney, it is celebrated by yacht racing.

At Christmas, the children pay little attention to Santa Claus. Instead they talk of Father Christmas, who comes by plane. Since December 25th may be the hottest day of the year for them, they may celebrate it on the beach.

January 26th is Australia's birthday, the day the first settlers landed. On April 25th, Anzac Day, something like our Veterans Day, is a time when Australians remember their brave soldiers. Anzac stands for Australia – New Zealand – Army Corps. The Queen of England's birthday, in June, is a time to express their loyalty to their mother country even though they are now a free nation.

Before you finish comparing holidays, the car stops beside a back gate.

"Here's our place," announces Kathy. Then her eye lights upon Jack, the kookaburra, sitting on the clothesline. "Look!" she exclaims. "There's our funny little jackass, about to laugh." Jackass is what Australians have nicknamed him.

As though he is telling the whole world how excited he is that you have arrived, kookaburra proudly throws back his head, chuckles, and then laughs hilariously. "HOOO HOOO HOOO," he begins slowly. Gradually he speeds up with tones that become sharper and shorter—"HAA HAA HAA HAA HOO HOO HOO HAA HAA HOO HOO HOO HA HA HA HA." On a rising note, he continues—"H! H! H! H! H! H! H! HOO HOO H! H! H! H!" . . . until you think he will burst. You break into a hearty laugh with him as the kookaburras in the nearby trees join in this delightful welcome to you.

KOOKABURRA

On the big porch in the front of the house, the children's mother serves you tea and delicious date scones which are something like English muffins. They are piping hot from her oven.

After tea, you go to a beach where waves break yards from shore. Yet even far out, the water is less than shoulder deep. The breakers roll to the white sandy beach in steady, foaming rows.

Kathy and Peter show you how to stand erect on a fast skimming board, and ride the crests of the waves. Around you, others are riding them in surf canoes. Farther out, water-skiers zip by. Australia has some of the world's most wonderful beaches and sea sports are a favorite activity. On this fine March day everybody is taking advantage of the last of the warm weather.

After your fun in the surf, you are ready for a rest and a good supper. Tonight there is lamb, rice and vegetables, with jello and custard sauce for dessert. Afterward, you have trouble keeping awake for television. You sleep very soundly that night.

KOALA

Next day you set out for Taronga Park Zoo. There you visit with animals from around the world but particularly with the ones that are native to Australia. Instead of being cooped in cages, most of the animals are fenced in natural surroundings like those from which they came. How glad you are that you brought your camera!

The zoo is set on a hill and you wander down a meandering path to meet the different animals. One of the zoo staff introduces you to a koala bear, a red kangaroo and an emu. He shows you how to hold the soft, furry koala, the most cuddly animal of the Australian bush. Then he places him in the fork of a sticky-barked, white gum tree. The koala spends most of his time here, sleeping or gazing down with a queer look of surprise. You see him chew on the gum leaves now and then, but never see him drink. He gets all the water he needs from his gum-leaf diet and the dew on the leaves. His name, koala, is an Aboriginal term meaning "no drink."

The kangaroo begs for some of your attention as he supports himself on his powerful hind legs and tail and brings his small front legs and deerlike head as close to the koala bear as possible. In the open country, he may grow as tall as a six-foot man and be able to leap 20 feet at a time with a speed of 30 miles an hour. It's hard to believe that he was only one inch long when he was born. His mother carried him in her pouch for three months until he was about a foot tall. Then for the next nine months he had a delightful life hopping in and out of her pouch. When his mother was in danger, she had to drop him, her joey as Australians call him, in the bush. Of course, she returned for him later. Finally, when his hind legs got too big for her pouch, joey had to learn to shift for himself.

KANGAROO

27

EMU

The emu holds himself proudly erect as he looks on. Next to the ostrich he is the world's largest non-flying bird. He can run 35 miles an hour and he is a strong swimmer besides. In the breeding season, he sits on the bottle-green eggs laid by his mate until odd-looking striped, whitish-gray chicks break through the shells.

Next, you search for the queer little platypus and his nearest living relative, the anteater. They are the only furred animals in existence that lay eggs.

Ah! There's the platypus —that peculiar beaverlike animal with a broad tail about six inches long, a ducklike bill, short legs and webbed feet ending in claws. He's about to dive for food in a near-by pool. You watch how hard he works his front legs. At the same time, he keeps his balance with the back ones and uses his tail as a rudder.

PLATYPUS

With eyes and ears closed, he nuzzles his soft rubbery bill around the muddy bottom of the pool. Now his cheek pouches are full, and he's coming to the top. He chews his catch, mud and all, and is ready for sleep. Strange as it may seem, to sleep he rolls himself into a ball and keeps his eyes open. What a funny little creature, this *boondaburra,* as Aboriginal legends call him. He's fish, bird and animal all in one.

In the distance, a little animal with many quills raises himself against a white wall. He's the anteater, thrusting out his long, sticky tongue to attract insects. His ancestors roamed the world with the dinosaurs millions of years ago.

Strolling along the path, you see a beautiful clock of flowers set in the ground. It actually keeps time. The works are hidden underneath. Talking birds distract your attention from the clock. Striking black, gray, scarlet, silvery-gray and pink-feathered cockatoos screech at you. Crimson, scarlet, blue, green and yellow parrots prattle loudly. In contrast, the budgerigar, Australian lovebird, speaks to you in a quaint, tiny voice.

LYREBIRD

Suddenly you think you hear the toot of a motor bus, but there's no bus in sight. You're listening to a great mimic, the lyrebird, putting on a unique song and dance performance. Through the silvery shower of his quivering, shivering feathers, he watches the mate he is trying to impress.

What an extraordinary tail! His feathers are flattened on each side of him. Two wirelike ones curl proudly upward, while other silvery plumes spread forward over his body. His gorgeous tail, of sixteen feathers altogether, is the pride of the family. It looks just like a lyre and the bird can sound like one, too, if he chooses. He pours out the glorious strains of his song — his own notes as well as imitations of the songs of other birds and sounds of things around him. He puts on a smart dance by stepping to one side, back again, and then giving a neat little hop. His mate may not admit it, but she's very pleased.

Now from the distance comes a sharp, barking note. A fairy penguin has been disturbed. He's a tiny member of the penguin family.

Some sleek, black swans cruise by. Their bodies are sunk in the water except for periscopelike necks and red-beaked heads.

BLACK SWAN

PELICAN

Waddling awkwardly on the bank are the pelicans. Who would guess they could be so graceful in the water and in flight?

The next day Kathy and Peter have another treat in store for you. It's the Royal Show. In Sydney, during Easter Week, more than a million people keep the show's turnstiles clicking.

Peter and Kathy take you from place to place to see the side shows, ring and trotting events, and pedigreed bulls. You watch the schedule carefully so you don't miss the contest in woodcutting. At last it's time for it to begin.

Wooden poles are set up like trees in a row. When the signal is given, one man on each team begins chopping at the top of that team's pole. Others take over, one by one, until the poles have been chopped down to the ground. How thrilling to watch these strong and nimble men of the bush! In the uniforms of their teams, they make the big chips fly in keen rivalry to have their team be "first through." Sure enough, the team you rooted for is the winner.

You go next to the huge Agricultural Hall. There the produce of the country is piled in rich and glowing patterns. There are pink-cheeked peaches and rows of apples — shiny red Jonathans and ripe green Granny Smiths. Pears come from the colder table-lands and oranges from nearby orchards, while pineapples, papayas and bananas come from the subtropical Queensland border. Grain wheat and wheat sheaves add to the beauty of the display. In another area are jars of honey and jam. What seems an endless variety of melons is piled next to giant pumpkins that weigh over a hundred pounds.

Peter is impatient to rush to the grandstand. The biggest feature of the show comes each day at three o'clock. It's the Grand Parade of thoroughbred horses and cattle.

Soon the cavalcade emerges through white gates into a grassy ring. Expert judges from Australia, Scotland, England and the United States cast sharp eyes on the approaching animals. First come the red-coated marshals on superb grays. They are followed by mounted police, stockmen with broad-brimmed hats, white moleskins over their shoulders, and pennant-tipped lances. Then come lines of men and women riders.

Now the real aristocrats of the show, guided by men or boys, are beginning to appear. There is a long, slow, moving tide of powerful, perfectly groomed bulls, stud cows, heifers and horses. Round and round the huge arena march all kinds of cattle breeds, each a champion in his class, each gaily bedecked with bright sashes and ribbons.

When the gay times of Easter vacation are over, Kathy takes you to school with her. In New South Wales, where she lives, all children must go to school until they are fifteen. In Tasmania even sixteen-year-olds must attend school. Each state has its own regulations about education. School starts in February rather than September and closes just before Christmas.

Dressed in the uniform of the school she attends, Kathy picks up her bag of books and the two of you are on your way. Her school, with grades from three through six, is called a primary school. Unlike more old-fashioned Australian schools, it's for both boys and girls.

At school Kathy introduces you to the headmaster or principal, to her teacher, and her sixth-grade classmates. The pupils study much the same subjects that you do. The classroom looks like yours too, but it's not centrally heated. The teacher may build a fire if the weather turns cold.

Lessons are serious affairs, and sober faces dot the classroom. Children do a lot of writing. Notebooks are neat and exact, and handwriting must be nearly perfect. Fortunately for the children, an occasional radio or television program brings relief from writing. Today the program tells an interesting story about squatters. Sometimes a week or two at a national fitness camp may also perk up the school schedule. Often a few parents come along to camp, too.

In the assembly hall, children sit on the floor. It's Kathy's day to read the Bible. How well she does it! She has practiced for the occasion. The children sing some of their favorite Australian bush songs. One class puts on a program to demonstrate how to use the telephone. Then the children file back to classes.

Outdoors, you can hear the school band practicing. There's a busy hum around the headmaster's office. Children are bringing donations for the big school bazaar. They must raise money for many purposes, including the cost of most of their books.

On the way home from school, you meet Peter and his friend Bob. They are returning from a boys' high school. When he graduates, Peter will get his *leaving certificate*. Then he will go to a university and study to be an engineer. There is a university in the capital city of each state as well as in the nation's capital at Canberra. Peter will get checks from the government while he attends college, just as though he were working. When he graduates, he would like to build bridges from fine Australian steel.

Bob wants to attend a technical school to learn how to lay television cables. Australia is much in need of trained technicians. Bob has a sister in business school and another in a teachers' college. His younger brother doesn't take to studying very well, so the school is organizing simpler courses for boys like him.

You would like to stay longer in Sydney but you are scheduled to see more of this great continent. When you say goodbye to Peter and Kathy, your flight takes you south to the little island of Tasmania.

Hobart, the capital city, is built on a fine harbor. Life there is unhurried and serene. Gums, laurel, wattles, myrtles and the ornamental celery-top pines, a hundred feet tall, cover slopes and valleys. But, alas, in this fairyland of beauty, the Tasmanian devil prowls. He has jet-black fur, with white markings, a nasty snoot, strong teeth and fiery eyes. A savage, snarling animal, he gorges himself on young and tender sheep.

In Tasmania's highlands, great lakes feed hydroelectric plants. The plants provide power for the only paper mills in the world that produce pulp for newspapers from hardwood.

Today there is no native population left in Tasmania. Natives were different there from those on the mainland. The Tasmanian natives were the living images of prehistoric cavemen. It's thought that they might have been driven to Tasmania from the mainland of Australia when the Aborigines arrived. In wars against them, 4,000 of the Tasmanians dwindled to 200. These were sent to Flinders, a lonely island off Tasmania's coast. There, tuberculosis wiped out the last of these mysterious people.

From Tasmania you fly to Melbourne, the capital of the state of Victoria. The city stands on the banks of the Yarra River, in the midst of sheep-grazing land. It is a great center for art. Artists set up many exhibits of their paintings, poets share their poetry, musicians give concerts in Town Hall, and actors produce some of the world's best plays.

Geoffrey, a boy whom you meet with his parents at your hotel, takes you to a fast Melbourne football game. It's played by eighteen men. Over the length of the field, opposing players are grouped in pairs instead of in line formation. They make long and accurate kicks, but do no tackling.

After the game, Geoffrey's parents invite you to their sheep station. It is sheep-shearing time, the busiest time of the year. Arriving by car and truck, the shearers quickly set up their stands in big sheds. With electric clippers, something like large electric razors, they work at great speed, shearing as many as 4,000 sheep in a day.

The fleeces are picked up by shed hands, carried to rolling tables, skirted and rolled. Skirting a fleece is removing patches, usually on the edge or "skirt," that don't match the rest. A wool classer can tell the quality and length of every fiber at a glance. After compressing the fleece in a big press and binding it in bales, the shearers pack up to move on to the next station.

Of course, Geoffrey is disappointed that you can't stay for the big celebration that follows — the dances, the picnic, the horse racing. But he helps you get a ride with the sheep shearers to the outskirts of Melbourne.

From Melbourne a short flight northward over the glistening, snow-capped Australian Alps brings you to the small town of Cooma. Eager to reach the snowy peaks, you travel by bus to Mt. Kosciusko, Australia's highest mountain. It is 7,328 feet high and cloaked in snow about six months of the year.

Suddenly an observant bus companion shouts, "Look! The kangaroos!" Sure enough, at least a half dozen kangaroos are making their great, long leaps through the bush. They are leaving the hills to find protection from the blizzards, hail and gales.

As you approach Cabramurra, Australia's highest town, 4,880 feet above sea level, you join the bus passengers in singing "Snowy River Roll." The song is about the great Snowy River dam and power project. The snow-fed water of the Snowy River, which flows directly to the ocean, is being dammed on the eastern side of the Great Dividing Range. Then it is turned westward through tunnels in the mountains to the Murray and Murrumbidgee Rivers. In this way, water that would otherwise be wasted is used to produce electricity and irrigate the dry plains of the interior. Started in 1949, operation Snowy River is scheduled to be finished in 1975.

In the cafeteria in Cabramurra, you join engineers, geologists, physicists, soil and water specialists and many other kinds of scientists and workers when their day's work is done. At one table there is great excitement tonight. A farewell party is under way for a young man who has been given a special award to study dam and tunnel building in the U.S.A.

The government leaders, who control the project, work in the nation's capital at Canberra. This garden city, designed by a Chicago architect, lies in a broad valley near the foothills of the Australian Alps. Canberra isn't in any Australian state. It's a territory by itself, something like Washington, D.C.

As you fly over it, you see the Australian flag waving on the Parliament building below you. In one corner of the flag, the Union Jack, Great Britain's symbol, shows that Australia is a member of the British Commonwealth of Nations. The Southern Cross is an Australian national symbol. There are six seven-pointed stars. They stand for the six Australian states. The seven points on each star represent the states and two territories, Canberra and the Northern Territory.

Your flight destination is the extreme northeastern part of the continent. There, for 1,500 miles, the Great Barrier Reef stretches from north to south along the shores of Queensland.

Off the reef swim tuna of unbelievable size, giant pike, and other fish weighing as much as 670 pounds. In dugout canoes made from the trunks of gum trees, Aborigines go after the fish with spears. They catch them with a faultless aim.

At the world-famous Underwater Coral Gardens Observatory, you gaze through porthole after porthole at some of the most beautiful and unusual fish in the world. They glide gracefully through coral branches and clumps. There are graceful shrimp banded with rainbow colors, striped orange and blue harlequin tusk fish, green frogfish and bottle-nosed blue dolphins. Huge sea anemones, three or four feet in width, wave their soft tentacles. Jellyfish float lazily by. A clam at least a yard wide opens and closes its jaws within a foot of you.

Now and then an octopus creeps out of an underwater cavern. How fascinating it seems as it changes color to suit the changing color of the reef! And over there on a sandbank lies a great, lazy, green turtle.

On the eastern face of the reef the struggle for life goes on endlessly, undisturbed, as it has for eons of time. A starfish wraps its arms around a shellfish, and a clam soon gobbles both of them. As evening comes, millions of sardine-type fish scatter before shoals of mackerel have a chance to devour them.

Queensland is famous for more than its reef. Its capital, Brisbane,

BLUE DOLPHIN

is a great shipping and shipbuilding center. It leads all of the states in raising cattle for beef. Sheep are also raised. The state produces sugar, cotton, maize, tobacco, tropical fruits and bamboo. Uranium has boomed the new Queensland settlement of Mary Kathleen. Abundant copper, lead and zinc make Mount Isa important. Great forests, large coal and bauxite deposits further add to Queensland's natural wealth.

Some of the state is heavily wooded jungleland. There are many curious trees and rare plants. The cycad, a bunch of fern that looks like string sprouting from a stubby, thick trunk, is a survivor of prehistoric plant life. A stinging nettle tree will punish you if you are unlucky enough to brush against any of its leaves, but close by, you will find a cunjevoy lily to cure your troubles. The juice of its stem or its two-foot-long spearlike leaves will kill the pain.

The lily grows in the shade of the twisting banyan. The banyan branches spread out, then descend to the ground at right angles, forming a new trunk from which more branches spread and drop. In this way, one tree may cover as much as half an acre. It looks like a half acre of jungle gym.

43

ADDER

You move cautiously through the jungle areas, remembering snakes you saw along the way — especially a four-foot brown snake stretched full-length across the road. He is a real killer, and many like him grow to seven or eight feet in length. The death adder is interesting to hear about, but who would like to meet him? He lies curled in a horseshoe shape with his tail in front of his mouth. He wiggles a yellowish-white appendage on his tail to attract lizards and birds. They think it's a worm, but they find out differently when the adder's long fangs inject a poison that stops their breath.

The carpet snake is harmless and useful. In this part of the country, people keep carpet snakes in the barn to eat rats and mice, much as you would keep a cat.

West of Queensland lies the Northern Territory. Part of it is "Never-Never Land," the great wilderness of barren mountains, sand and salt beds that challenged early explorers. Part is jungle. A section of it, Arnhem Land, has been set aside as a reservation for the Aborigines. The Australian Government, however, doesn't consider the reservation — or other centers for Aborigines elsewhere — as permanent. The government aim is to educate these first Australians to live and work with all other citizens.

The chief towns of the Northern Territory are Darwin, a small seaport, and Alice Springs, a tourist center. To "the Alice," people flock from all parts by plane, automobile, train or bus.

Some of the people of the town have made a hobby of collecting native Aboriginal art, and other Australian specialities. You are invited to their homes to see these treasures. Some are for sale and you may bring them home as souvenirs.

You examine a boomerang, the curved weapon that will return to the hand of its thrower. You shiver a little at the sight of a sharp, pointed stone attached to a wooden handle by a mixture of clay and human blood. This gory tool was used by Stone Age people in a ceremony which marked the time when young boys were considered to have grown up. The veins of the men of the tribe were cut to let the blood flow over the bodies of the boys.

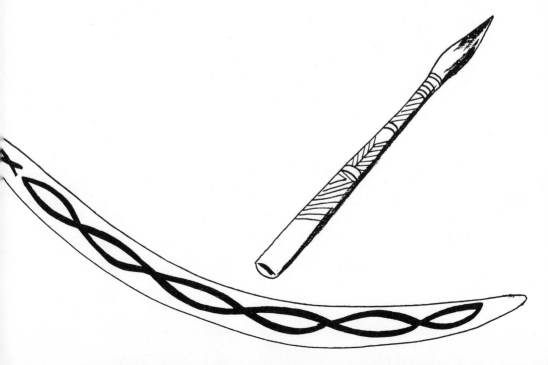

You admire a display of precious and semiprecious stones: diamonds, sapphires, emeralds, rubies, aquamarines, topaz, zircon, garnets, amethysts, onyx and jasper. You select a black opal as a souvenir. These fiery stones have gray or black bases. Yours flashes deep flames of fire in the midst of velvety greens, blues and reds.

The Alice is also the exciting headquarters of the Flying Doctor Service. The Service operates twelve medical bases linked by two-way radio to more than 1,000 outpost regions. By means of a radio transceiver, a person talks with a faraway doctor, tells what trouble he is having, and learns what to do about it. Electricity to send the message is made just by pushing the transceiver's pedals. If necessary, a doctor or nurse will fly to the sick free of charge.

Homesteads built far from civilization all have runways in their yards to enable planes to land. Not only doctors and nurses, but mailmen use the runway. How lucky you are that tomorrow a mailman will take you on his rounds!

Very early, as the first brilliant rays of the sun begin to shine on the sandy earth, you reach the airport. Scattered about are little planes, ready to jump from station to station like wild kangaroos. The mailman points out the Flying Doctor's plane and then leads you to a single-engine Cessna. Over mountains, plains and salt beds you fly. Occasionally your pilot-mailman flies low enough for you to take a good look at camel tracks in the sand. Finally, you catch up with the camels.

After several stops to deliver mail and refuel, your mailman deposits you along with his letters. You are going to set out by bus for a cattle station. On the way, your guide builds a fire in a dried-up river bed and boils a *billy* — a tin can — of tea. Along with it, he chars to juicy crispness a thick filet mignon steak — the best you ever tasted. You sit down to enjoy the spread on banks of red sand glistening with mica.

As you continue your journey, you notice many mulga trees. This scrubby hardwood polishes beautifully and is used to make ornamental objects. You also see cork trees that get their name from their corklike bark. The drooping ironwood trees remind you of willows. The wild orange tree bears fruit the size of a golf ball. On vines that trail along the ground grow poisonous, lemonlike melons.

The ghostlike gum trees are the most impressive of all, especially one that is 13 feet around and 600 years old. Its snow-white bark covers a trunk which yields a sticky resin. In addition to the white gums, Australia has blue and red gums — 365 varieties of them.

You pass a hermit's broken-down lodge where your driver pauses long enough to drop off a bit of food for the man. He lives near an abandoned town that flourished during the gold rush. Little remains but the police station, shells of a few houses, and old rusty machinery.

Now you approach one of the homesteads at the cattle station. This is an old homestead that has been lived in for four generations. It's one of two on the station's 1,400 square miles of land. In this vast area wire fences enclose 2,000 horses and 7,000 head of cattle in huge paddocks. The paddocks are so big that boundary riders who watch over the cattle have to carry camping gear.

You are delighted to find newly built cabins for visitors to the station. Covered with sand of the desert, you head for the shower. You're ready for bed as soon as you have had dinner.

Next morning, a parade of children from two families greets you as you leave your cabin. They have brought their favorite pets along with them. There's Tom, Geoffrey, Joe, Andy, Jane, and Mary — with Kim, the favorite sheep dog. Willy, the billy goat, bounds ahead through the garden like a big brute. Each child takes turns carrying Nanny, the young goat. Snuffy, the cat, brings up the rear.

The children have come to take you around. With pride they point to the swimming pool that will soon be ready to use. A big windmill pumps water from the Great Artesian Basin beneath the surface. The boys insist you visit their favorite spot: the mechanic's workshop. It has plenty of tools, spare parts and odds and ends to tinker with.

The children introduce you to Sam, the Aboriginal stockman. He has been hard at work for months branding the cattle with the mark of the owner. This mark enables a station manager to recognize his own cattle. It also makes stealing more difficult for the thieves who try to cart off cattle in their trailer trucks. Cattle stealing is called *cattle-duffing* or *poddy-dodging*. Poddies are hard to identify because they are young, unbranded beasts, but if a policeman catches a thief with branded animals he can tell where to return them.

Today Sam is helping round up cattle for the annual turnoff. With cheerful cries and cracking of whips, stockmen bring in the last ones to be driven to market.

Now *overlanding* begins. That's driving the herd to the nearest *railhead* — or railway. It's only 48 miles away but it will take four days to get there, because cows can travel only about 12 miles a day. From some of the more remote stations, cows must be driven as far as 1,000 miles. In that case, they may lose so much weight that they have to be grazed for weeks at the end of the trip before they are sold.

You watch the herd wind out of sight. You wish you could remain to see Sam tackle his next job: breaking in the wild horses, or *brumbies,* but time is flying. You have a date to explore some caves where long ago Australia's Aborigines lived.

In a sturdy bus, you jog over rocky, roadless desert. Suddenly the bus comes to a standstill. You are stranded in hot, red sand.

Your driver doesn't seem disturbed. He has met situations like this many times before. He pulls a radio transceiver from behind the back seat of the bus, places it on the sandy ground, and searches for the aerial. It's missing, but don't worry. Using odds and ends of wire from his scrap box, the driver makes a new one. Then he tries to tune in to send a telegram asking for help. But it's impossible — the School of the Air is in session.

A broken-down bus is not a sufficiently good reason for interrupting the broadcast, so this is your chance to listen over the transceiver to teachers and children in this new kind of school.

A teacher in a radio studio at Alice Springs talks with students as far as 500 miles from here, and the pupils reply. This morning the class is learning to write a letter. The teacher calls the roll to know which children are attending. She talks with them about the reasons for writing the letter and the form to use. Then one by one the pupils suggest sentences which they think should be included. When no one speaks up, the teacher says, "Well, I don't hear a word." When necessary, she calls on someone.

The School of the Air cooperates with a Correspondence School, which assigns and corrects homework. Once a year, the children may have a chance to go to Alice Springs to work in a regular class-room, face to face with their teacher. When they meet, pupils almost always recognize each other, and the teacher recognizes them from the sound of their voices!

This morning, school comes to an end with the teacher reading the poem of a pupil, Ann Chamberlain, which the Correspondence School published in its magazine:

RAIN

Rain, rain, come today,
Come and have a little stay.
Come now, rain, and break the drought;
Rain all day and night throughout.
Come and make the grasses grow,
And make the rivers rise and flow.
Come and lend a helping hand,
Bring brightness to the parched, dry land.

Marooned in the hot sand, you know just how Ann feels. Your guide still can't send his telegram. People must have a chance to talk to their doctors first. So you listen to the woman with the swollen leg and to the one with the sick baby. After the doctor gives them advice, your guide cuts in once more, giving his code: "9 Uncle Obo, 9UO; 9 Uncle Obo, 9UO; 9 Uncle Obo, 9UO."

At last, he hears "T Sugar," his signal to come in. Then he sends his radiogram to ask someone to bring a Volkswagen.

When the Volkswagen arrives, it takes you to a rocky bushland. You get out and climb over rocks and boulders much bigger than you are. No matter if you get tired, you must hustle to keep up with the group, so as not to get lost in this lonely stretch of land.

When you reach the cave for which you're heading, you find it

worth the effort. The walls are decorated with strange and fascinating Aboriginal drawings. Some are of kangaroos and hunters. Some are of *dingos,* or wild dogs. Others are legendary animals. Present-day Aborigines can't tell you what the animals mean. They have lost many of the tribal secrets of their ancestors.

After all the climbing and crawling, you're ready for the hearty meal that awaits you upon your return to the homestead.

That night the guests gather comfortably in the long living room. Your guide tells you a little about the Aborigines, men like Sam, who work at the station. They make their *mia mias,* or shelters, from trees and bushes. They don't like to build permanent homes. They prefer to move when a place gets dirty. They love to roam the country, to go *walkabout,* as they say.

Many of them have never learned to read or write, and in their kind of life they haven't needed to know much arithmetic. So they count to three, say *two-two* for four, and let five stand for many. Yet they have a kind of knowledge that unlocks nature's secrets. They can live when civilized men die for lack of food and water. They know every rock hole where water is to be obtained. They can drain moisture from the roots of trees and shrubs. They even get water from a frog that fills himself in the wet season. In fact, one of their famous folk tales is about a great fat frog that drank up all the water but lost it because of his own hearty laugh. A clever little eel worked hard to make the frog laugh by standing on his tail and wiggling for all he was worth.

These original Australians, the Aborigines, are a people of contrasting ways. They can be both brutal and kindhearted. Bearded warriors, keeping to rules their father made, have often waged savage war to protect ancestral hunting grounds. Naturally, it has been hard for them to understand why a white newcomer can take *their* kangaroos when *they* can't take *his* sheep!

ABORIGINE

56

Sometimes they beat their wives unmercifully. On the other hand, they are extremely good to children and care for the blind with great tenderness. In this country, bright sun and sand are very hard on the eyes. Many of the Aborigines have watery eyes. Unless they report to the local medical office regularly, they are likely to become blind.

They can be gay as well as serious. On your way back to Alice Springs, your guide gives you a chance to watch some of their gaiety. It's a *corroboree,* an Aboriginal camp dance. The families sit in a ring around the campfire as the music begins. The first musician makes a few moaning blasts on a hollow bamboo horn, a *didjerido.* Then come deep, droning notes. Another player keeps time by beating two hard pieces of wood together. Suddenly, with a hoarse, yelping voice, he bursts into song.

A few old women move closer toward the fire and sit down cross-legged. They clap their cupped hands vigorously. Try it yourself and you will hear a hollow, drumlike sound. Soon the air vibrates with the drumming beat, the chant of male voices, the clicking of dry sticks, and the drone of the horn.

57

From time to time there is solo dancing in the center of the ring. After each dance, the music stops abruptly. Everyone bursts into loud rejoicings. They smoke, chat, and then begin the music and dancing again.

"This merrymaking will continue far into the night," your guide explains. But you must be on your way.

Back at Alice Springs, you meet men from another pioneering area, Rum Jungle. There uranium is being mined and extracted from radioactive ore. The miners tell you something about their land. Its countryside is a great contrast to the desert. Rivers, cascades and waterfalls keep it green. Thousands of buffaloes gallop over plains and swamps. Hundreds of crocodiles lurk in the Alligator River. Wild geese and duck abound.

Aboriginal paintings on the cliffs are fascinating. One is on a slab hundreds of feet above the valley. How the artists climbed and stood there to paint remains a mystery. Many of the paintings are called X-ray paintings. For instance, a fish can be seen passing behind a larger fish so that one fish is viewed through the body of the other. While the government and private charitable organizations are trying to help Aborigines learn modern ways, they also hope to help them preserve the secrets of such historic crafts.

Before leaving the land of the Aborigines for Australia's far west, you take a look at the state of Southern Australia. It's a belt of rich vineyards, rolling mountains and sunny beaches. Adelaide, its capital, is a manufacturing center.

From Adelaide to Perth, the capital of Western Australia, you travel in an air-conditioned coach. For 330 miles your train runs without making a single curve. You pass few towns, except the settlements of gold miners. Western Australia, which produces most of Australia's gold, takes up almost a third of the continent. But most of the land is too dry to live on. That's why half of the people of the state live in Perth.

Flying north from Perth for a thousand miles, you land at the town of Broome, a pearling base. Two pearlers meet you and take you to their luggers, or boats. They show you the outfits they wear when they dive for mother-of-pearl.

There is a corselet, big boots and heavy underwear. There is a helmet with three windows, a center one and one on either side. A lifeline and air hose connect the diver with his lugger. He breathes through the air hose. The lifeline tows him, in a slanted position, just above the bottom of the sea.

He must be alert every moment he is down there. He watches closely for fish that can help or harm him. For instance, a chinafish may serve as a faithful guide to lead him right into a patch of the mussel, clam or other shelled creatures that secrete mother-of-pearl. The same conditions that encourage the growth of mother-of-pearl favor the life of the chinafish, so the fish hangs around the pearl.

When the diver sights a shell, he signals with his lifeline. Aboard the lugger, a man called a tender lets out the hose and line. The diver lets some air out of his helmet and sinks down to the shell. As he approaches, a little sentinel, such as a tiny crab or crayfish, scuttles into the shell, and the shell closes.

The diver must be on the lookout not only for sentinels but for sharks, whales, horrid diamond fish and giant groupers.

The whales can interfere with his air hose and lifeline. The diamond fish, which weighs several tons, generally sleeps on the ocean floor. But when disturbed, he rises and charges like a bull with his V-shaped horns. The giant grouper, with his enormous head and mouth, can swallow a diver up to the armpits.

Look there! A lugger is returning from sea. As the men bring in their load of shells, crewmen sort, grade, clean and pack them for shipment to the United States, France, Italy and England. There the lustrous inner coating is made into buttons, buckles, necklaces, handles for knives, finger boards of musical instruments and compass dials, among other things.

Does it seem a long way from this pearl diving base to your home town? After you go back to Perth, a modern jet will take you to the middle of the U.S.A. in less than a day and a half. What a contrast to the eight months spent by the early settlers sailing to Sydney from England!

During your flight home, you wonder what the future of Australia, sometimes called the Crossroads of the World, will be. Will pioneering engineers be able to turn the desert into farmland? Will they produce electric power for industries that might support millions more people? If this should happen, will people then come to spacious Australia from overcrowded lands in Asia? If so, how will the new and old Australians get along? Will the oldest Australians, the Aborigines, become more blended in the population than they are now?

Now that you know Australia's past and present, you will want to watch its future. And perhaps upon arriving home, you'll want to pass along to your friends the invitation of Australian boys and girls to visit them at work and play. In fact, why not ask children of the world to join in a hearty laugh of friendship with Jack, the kookaburra?

HOW TO PRONOUNCE WORDS AND NAMES "DOWN UNDER"

Word	Pronunciation	Word	Pronunciation
Aborigines	*Ab*-or-*ij*-ee-nees	emu	*ee*-mew
boondaburra	*boon*-dah-*bur*-rah	koala	koh-*ah*-lah
brumbies	*brum*-bees	kookaburra	*koo*-kah-*bur*-ah
budgerigar	*bud*-jer-*ree*-jah	mia mias	*mee*-ah *mee*-ahs
Cabramurra	*Kah*-brah-*mur*-ah	Murrumbidgee	*Mur*-um-*bid*-gee
Canberra	*Kan*-brah	platypus	*plat*-ee-puss
corroboree	koh-*rob*-or-ee	warra warra	*war*-ah *war*-ah

HISTORY

1606—A Dutch vessel, the *Duyfken,* made the first recorded trip to Australia.

1770—Captain Cook claimed New South Wales for Britain.

1778—Captain Phillip, with 1,000 convicts and soldiers from England, settled at Sydney Cover.

1786–1825—Colonists settled in New South Wales and Tasmania.

1827—England claimed all of Australia as British Territory.

1829–1834—British settlers arrived in Western and South Australia.

1851—Victoria became a British Colony. Gold was discovered.

1855—In the Australian Colonies Government Act, the British Government gave the five colonies the right to set up their own constitutions.

1859—Queensland became the sixth British Colony in Australia.

1901—January 1st. The Commonwealth of Australia was proclaimed.

1911—Canberra, the site of the national capital, became Australian Capital Territory. Northern Territory came under the Commonwealth Government.

1914–18—Australians fought with the British and their allies in World War I. Their Expeditionary Force occupied New Guinea.

1920—Queensland and Northern Territory Aerial Services, Qantas, were organized.

1931—Australia became an independent dominion within the British Commonwealth.

1939–45—Australians fought in World War II. They perfected methods of jungle warfare when the Japanese attacked them in the north.

1946—By United Nations Trusteeship Agreement, Papua and New Guinea as well as some small islands in the Pacific were placed in the care of Australia.

1947—Australia joined the United Nations. The Commonwealth Government bought the Qantas Company.

1949—The Snowy River scheme began to divert and store water for irrigation and electric power.

1950—Australia entered into the Colombo Plan to aid countries of Asia.

1951—The Anzus Pact was signed.

1952—Qantas opened the first air route across the Indian Ocean.

1954—Australia entered into the SEATO agreement.

1956—Television was introduced to Sydney and Melbourne.

1962—Australians in Perth turned on their lights as a signal to America's first man in orbit. The Mayor of Perth came to New York to participate in the parade which followed.

Australia works to develop its educational system, assimilate its Aboriginal population and make the dry third of its land habitable. Continues to play an important role in world affairs. Emphasis on industrial development and research is growing, especially in steel, chemicals, paper and plastics. A search for oil continues.

INDEX

THE GETTING TO KNOW BOOKS

COVER TODAY'S WORLD

GETTING TO KNOW
　　AFRICA'S FRENCH COMMUNITY

GETTING TO KNOW ALASKA

GETTING TO KNOW THE ARCTIC

GETTING TO KNOW ARGENTINA

GETTING TO KNOW AUSTRALIA

GETTING TO KNOW BRAZIL

GETTING TO KNOW
　　　　BRITISH WEST INDIES

GETTING TO KNOW BURMA

GETTING TO KNOW CANADA

GETTING TO KNOW CHILE

GETTING TO KNOW CUBA

GETTING TO KNOW EGYPT, U.A.R.

GETTING TO KNOW F.A.O.

GETTING TO KNOW FRANCE

GETTING TO KNOW GERMANY

GETTING TO KNOW GREECE

GETTING TO KNOW HAWAII

GETTING TO KNOW HONG KONG

GETTING TO KNOW
　THE HUMAN RIGHTS COMMISSION

GETTING TO KNOW INDIA

GETTING TO KNOW INDONESIA

GETTING TO KNOW ISRAEL

GETTING TO KNOW ITALY

GETTING TO KNOW JAPAN

GETTING TO KNOW KOREA

GETTING TO KNOW LEBANON

GETTING TO KNOW LIBERIA

GETTING TO KNOW MALAYA

GETTING TO KNOW MEXICO

GETTING TO KNOW NIGERIA

GETTING TO KNOW PAKISTAN

GETTING TO KNOW PANAMA

GETTING TO KNOW THE PHILIPPINES

GETTING TO KNOW POLAND

GETTING TO KNOW PUERTO RICO

GETTING TO KNOW SOUTH PACIFIC

GETTING TO KNOW SPAIN

GETTING TO KNOW SWITZERLAND

GETTING TO KNOW TANGANYIKA

GETTING TO KNOW THAILAND

GETTING TO KNOW TURKEY

GETTING TO KNOW THE
　　　　　　TWO CHINAS

GETTING TO KNOW
　　UNITED NATIONS CRUSADERS

GETTING TO KNOW UNESCO

GETTING TO KNOW THE U.S.S.R.

GETTING TO KNOW VENEZUELA

GETTING TO KNOW THE
　　　　　　VIRGIN ISLANDS